Nature Watch
Dangerous Animals

CONTENTS

What is a dangerous animal?	2
Types of danger	4
Crocodiles: big biters	6
Snapping turtles & sea snakes	8
Sharks: top predators	10
Slashes, shocks & toxins	12
Fish that sting	14
Little nippers!	16
Suckers & "shells"	18
Tentacles of terror	20
Pretty but prickly	22
Frogs, toads, yabbies & more	24
Snapping or squeezing	26
Snakes: deadly biters	28
Dangerous in doses	30
Feathered fury	32
Small but deadly	34
Boxing, biting & stampeding	36
Cats, rats & bats	38
Attack from the air…	40
Disease in flight	42
Small but painful stingers	44
How to help yourself	46
Glossary	48

INTRODUCTION

Lionfish

What is a dangerous animal?

Dusky whaler shark

Australia has many dangerous and deadly animals that can injure or kill humans. Most are simply protecting themselves from danger when they bite or attack, but some see humans as a type of food. How dangerous an animal is depends on its size, its strength and the ways in which it attacks. Some animals can cause only small injuries and are mostly harmless, while others can kill.

Humans can be prey for some predators, but remember that animals eating each other is part of nature. Australia's oceans and rivers are home to sharks and, in the north, hungry crocodiles, which can see humans that enter their territory as dinner.

Other animals only attack in self-defence, and some injuries are caused by animals that are usually harmless. Male platypuses, for example, have a venomous spike on the hindleg that can hurt a human if a platypus is caught.

Platypus

Into the wild...

You shouldn't think of dangerous animals as mean, evil or savage. Instead, remember that "wild" animals are exactly that — wild — and they should all be treated carefully. Most wild animals are afraid of humans and may react to you with fright or anger.

Dingo

Most people would guess the crocodile is more dangerous than the kangaroo, but this is a freshwater crocodile, which has not been known to attack humans. However, there have been a number of attacks from kangaroos, which have caused awful injuries and even one death in the past.

Which is more dangerous?

Read the signs!

Most animals attack because they are scared or alarmed. Even then, many try to frighten an attacker away first with a "threat display". Threat displays may include raising a frill, puffing themselves up to look bigger, trying to hide, changing colour, or even, like snakes, flattening their necks or hissing and raising themselves up into position so they are ready to strike.

INTRODUCTION

Collett's snake

Types of danger

Bull ant

Dangerous animals may bite, sting, kick or even be toxic or poisonous if eaten, but it is important you remember that most animals would rather avoid humans than hurt them. Also remember that these animals have "weapons" not to harm humans but to help the animal survive.

White shark

Some animals look small and harmless but may be just as dangerous as larger animals like sharks. Although many people have died from bee stings and ant bites, which can cause allergic reactions, most people are not afraid of ants but are very scared of sharks.

Animals that spread disease

Itch mite

Can you guess the deadliest animal on Earth? It is the tiny mosquito. Mosquitoes are deadly because they can carry parasites and viruses that spread life-threatening diseases such as malaria, Ross River fever and dengue fever. Other types of insects also spread diseases that can infect humans if they are bitten, scratched or come into contact with the animal's poo or saliva. Other animals may have lice or mites that can cause illness or disease in humans.

ANIMALS THAT BITE, SCRATCH OR SPIKE

Some large animals are able to injure humans if they are hungry or angry. These animals include razor-toothed crocodiles, sharks and dingoes. They also include other animals that are mostly harmless but have caused deaths in the past, such as kangaroos and cassowaries. Other animals, like some fish and rays, have sharp spines or spikes that can cause wounds. Yet others swoop and scratch to scare humans away from their nests or homes.

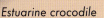
Estuarine crocodile

ANIMALS NOT TO EAT

Stars-and-stripes puffer

One of the best ways for animals to protect themselves from other animals that want to eat them is to be poisonous. Toxic or poisonous animals have chemicals in their bodies that can make their predators very sick. Many fish, like pufferfish, are poisonous to humans. Some crabs and toads are also poisonous.

ANIMALS WITH VENOM

Some animals that need to catch and control prey quickly produce venom — a powerful liquid that causes pain, paralysis or death. They use venom to sting or bite attackers or threats. Some, such as snakes and spiders, are able to inject venom into their victims by biting with their fangs. Others, like sea jellies, have stinging tentacles that they wrap around prey to kill it.

Box jelly

Animal attacks

Tiger shark

Deaths caused by animals are rare and are not even among the ten most common causes of death in Australia. Humans are more likely to die from heart disease, than from an animal attack.

IN OCEANS & RIVERS
CROCODILES

Freshwater crocodile

Crocodiles: big biters

Estuarine crocodiles are huge, ancient reptiles that can easily attack, drown and eat an adult human. However, their smaller cousins, freshwater crocodiles, have never been known to kill humans. As estuarine crocodiles have also been found in freshwater rivers, and some people may not be able to tell the two species apart, always pay attention to warning signs.

Estuarine crocodile eating a wallaby

Crocodiles can be hard to see because they look like floating logs. These clever reptiles can remember which paths people and animals take to the water. They lurk by known "drinking" spots at the water's edge, then rush out and attack.

Estuarine crocodile

Freshwater crocodile

Protect yourself

In Australia's north, which is "croc country", warning signs tell tourists and locals not to swim. But out-of-the-way beaches or camping spots might not have signs. If you are unsure, do not swim and stay away from the water's edge.

Estuarine crocodile

I am the largest, most deadly reptile!

Jumping giants

Crocodiles can move very quickly, both in and out of the water. They are able to leap up in the air to snatch up birds and bats that roost in trees above the water, but they also eat fish and other reptiles. Although they spend a lot of time in the water, they come to land to bask (or warm their blood) and lay their eggs.

Estuarine crocodile

IN OCEANS & RIVERS
TURTLES & SEA SNAKES

Olive sea snake

Snapping turtles & sea snakes

Other reptiles that live in oceans and rivers can cause injuries or death. Turtles may seem harmless, but they have tough beaks that can shear through flesh to give a nasty nip if disturbed. Sea snakes are more dangerous. Like their relatives, the venomous land snakes, they have powerful venom that can kill. Thankfully, most sea snakes are shy and rarely bite divers or swimmers.

Green turtle

Have you ever heard the term "snapping turtle"? It comes from the fact that some turtles have been known to "snap" or bite when handled. Australia has more than 40 types of turtle and all have strong jaws covered with bony plates. A bite from the larger marine species can even crush fingers and cause a painful wound.

Victoria River turtle

Toxic turtles

Marine turtles are now protected in Australia, but in the early 1900s, turtle soup was common in restaurants around Australia. It is a very bad idea to eat marine turtles because their flesh, and even their eggs, can have a build-up of toxins that can poison people.

Ranger and green turtle

Sea snake

Please only watch me and don't touch.

Turtle-headed Sea Snake

Snakes of the sea

Sea snakes are known to be curious about divers and snorkellers, but they are also rather gentle, shy snakes and very rarely bite. Most bites from sea snakes happen when anglers get them tangled on lines or in nets.

IN OCEANS & RIVERS
SHARKS

Bull shark

Sharks: top predators

Of course, the most feared predators of them all, sharks, also prowl rivers and oceans searching for prey. Sharks are incredibly fast and fierce, and their razor-sharp teeth even regrow when they fall out! Most sharks feed on fish, turtles, seals, sea-lions or other marine animals, but sometimes an unlucky human swimmer or surfer may be mistaken for prey.

Greynurse shark jawbone

Oceanic whitetip shark

Although sharks seem scary, we should respect them rather than fear them because, in fact, sharks are more at risk from us than we are from them. Every year humans kill and eat millions of sharks, but only about ten Australians a year are bitten by sharks and most survive.

White shark

Avoid attack

The best way to avoid a shark attack is to never swim alone, do not swim in murky water, do not swim at night, dawn or dusk, and never swim with pets. If you hear a shark alarm, don't panic — quickly swim to shore. If attacked by a shark, try to hit it as hard as possible on the snout or poke at its eyes.

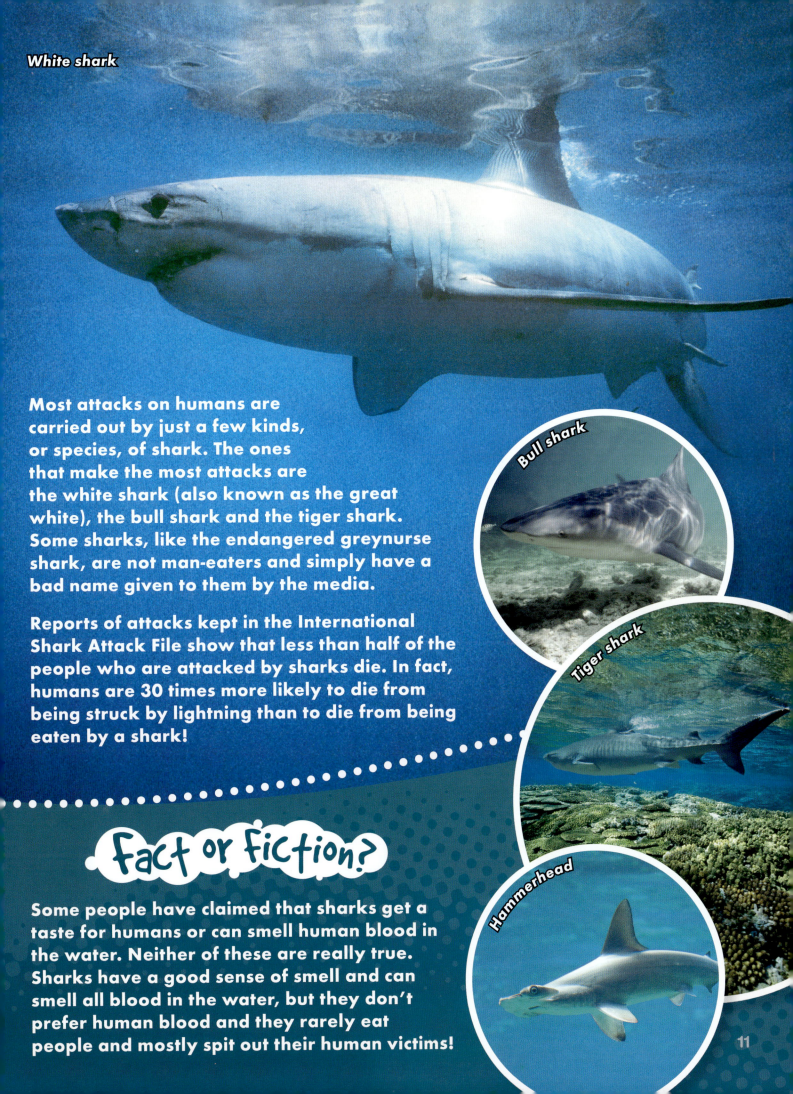

White shark

Bull shark

Tiger shark

Hammerhead

Most attacks on humans are carried out by just a few kinds, or species, of shark. The ones that make the most attacks are the white shark (also known as the great white), the bull shark and the tiger shark. Some sharks, like the endangered greynurse shark, are not man-eaters and simply have a bad name given to them by the media.

Reports of attacks kept in the International Shark Attack File show that less than half of the people who are attacked by sharks die. In fact, humans are 30 times more likely to die from being struck by lightning than to die from being eaten by a shark!

Fact or fiction?

Some people have claimed that sharks get a taste for humans or can smell human blood in the water. Neither of these are really true. Sharks have a good sense of smell and can smell all blood in the water, but they don't prefer human blood and they rarely eat people and mostly spit out their human victims!

IN OCEANS & RIVERS
FISH

Eel

Slashes, shocks & toxins

It might surprise you, but fish are some of the deadliest animals. They have many weapons of defence that can hurt humans or prey, including sharp, slashing spines, being poisonous or venomous, or even giving an electric shock!

Many fish have sharp fins or blade-like spikes, known as spines, that can slash through flesh if the fish is caught and handled. In some fish, these spines release venom that can cause intense pain or death to humans.

Some fish can also give a powerful bite. The great barracuda is a huge fish with a mouth full of long, sharp teeth. It can easily chomp off a person's hand and is known as the "tiger of the sea" because of its bite.

Red morwong

Eyestripe surgeonfish

Great barracuda

That's shocking!

Coffin ray

The coffin ray is an amazing fish that is able to create a weak electrical charge to shock its prey or attacker. The electric shock is enough to stun fish and can even knock a human over, but hasn't been known to kill anyone. They are called coffin rays because their shape looks a little like the shape of a coffin, but they are also known as numbfish or electric rays.

Most humans like to eat fish, but not all fish can be eaten safely. Many large fish, especially tropical ones, get a build-up of toxins in their bodies from feeding on smaller fish. This can lead to a type of poisoning in humans if they eat these toxic fish. Large mackerel, chinamenfish and coral trout have been known to contain this toxin.

Spanish mackerel

Chinamanfish

There's something fishy about my flesh!

Poison Puffs

Pufferfish also have a deadly toxin in their bodies and eating just a small amount of their flesh or skin can kill. In Japan, some people believe the flesh of the pufferfish, which they call *"fugu"*, is a delicacy, and special chefs prepare it for diners. However, many people have died from eating *fugu*.

Threebar porcupinefish

IN OCEANS & RIVERS
VENOMOUS FISH

Estuarine stonefish

Fish that sting

Some of the deadliest fish are the venomous fish. These fish have sharp spines that inject venom into their prey or into the feet of people who step on them. Some of them can kill within minutes.

Australian waters are home to the most dangerous fish of all — the reef stonefish. Stings from it and from its relative the estuarine stonefish can cause extreme pain, paralysis and death very quickly.

Common lionfish

Reef stonefish

False stonefish

Demon stingerfish

Stone or scorpion?

Most venomous fish belong to the scorpionfish family. Their skin colours, fins, spines and speckles help them blend in with the sea floor or with reef coral. Scorpionfish, such as the false stonefish and demon stingerfish, use their venom to fend off attackers while they ambush prey on the sea bottom.

Stingrays are the largest venomous fish in Australian waters. A barbed "sting" at the end of a stingray's tail can cause a painful wound. While some people have died from being stabbed with a stingray tail, a ray's venom is more painful than truly deadly.

Striped stingaree

Banded stingray

Stingray barb

Port Jackson shark fin

Knife-like fins

Some small bottom-living sharks also have venomous spines. Young Port Jackson sharks have a knife-like venomous spine on the top fin. Spines and barbs such as these cause dangerous flesh wounds that, if near the heart or organs, could be deadly.

IN OCEANS & RIVERS
INVERTEBRATES

Little nippers!

Crabs, lobsters and yabbies use their strong front claws to pinch off pieces of food or hold struggling prey, as well as to fight each other. Their "nippers", once they latch on to something, can be very hard to get off and can cause awful, pinching pain.

Crab

Banded mantis shrimp

Ghost shrimp

Mantis shrimps and yabbies, which are a type of ghost shrimp, also have nipping claws. Most are small but they can grow up to 30 centimetres long (as long as a ruler). They are known as "thumbsplitters" because they nip or flick their spiny bodies to split skin.

Fierce fronts

Mud crab

Crabs scuttle rather slowly, so animals like the mud crab need protective front claws that can scare away threats. While their pincers can crush fingers, they are only able to attack from the front. Their back legs, behind the tough shell, have no claws at all.

Devil crab

Aside from nipping, some crabs are also dangerous to humans by being poisonous. Just a tiny nibble of the flesh of the devil crab, which lives on coral reefs through the Pacific and Indian Oceans, is enough to kill a human. So if you don't know whether the species of crab you have caught is safe, don't eat it.

I make a deadly, devilish dinner!

Clamming up

Cartoons and old sailor's tales sometimes make believe that giant clams are able to snap their shells shut on a diver's legs. This is untrue. Giant clams close their shells very slowly and are not a threat to humans at all.

Giant clam

IN OCEANS & RIVERS
OCTOPUSES & "SHELLS"

Suckers & "shells"

Southern sand octopus

Octopuses, cone shells and other molluscs use a range of different tactics, or tricks, to kill threats or get food. The blue-ringed octopus may look beautiful, but its bright colours are a warning to stay away because it is venomous. Other marine molluscs, like cone shells which are a type of sea slug, may be protected by a hard shell, but they also have venom to help them kill prey and attack intruders.

Gloomy octopus

Scientists recently found out that all octopuses, squid and cuttlefish are venomous, but most of them are not able to inject venom into humans as successfully as the deadly blue-ringed octopus. Instead, they use it to kill prey. Despite that, a giant cuttlefish can still give a nasty bite because it has a sharp, beak-like mouth. However, stories about giant squid wrapping their tentacles around boats and sinking them are just tall tales.

A sluggish killer

Giant cuttlefish

Cone shell

They may look just like beautiful patterned shells, but cone shells are deadly. These meat-eaters poke a harpoon-like proboscis (or nose) out of the thin end of the shell. It has sharp teeth that inject venom into its victim.

Southern blue-ringed octopus

Blue-ringed octopuses are among the most venomous animals on the planet and Australia has seven species. When an octopus is under attack, bright blue rings flash all over its body, warning the attacker that they risk being bitten. The venom acts quickly and is very painful, causing paralysis (which means being unable to move), vomiting and death. There is no cure for the venom.

Polluting poisons

Many people think oysters, scallops and other shelled molluscs are delicious, but some of them can build up toxic chemicals or bacteria (tiny, germ-like creatures) if they grow in polluted water. Eating polluted shellfish can cause allergies, severe illness or death.

Oyster

Oyster farm

IN OCEANS & RIVERS
VENOMOUS INVERTEBRATES

Tentacles of terror

Sea anemone

Animals that move slowly or stay in one spot are even more in need of ways to get rid of predators. For this reason, many sea creatures that attach themselves to the bottom or to coral are venomous. Others, like sea jellies, are slow swimmers that must kill their prey before it swims away. They have very strong venom and sometimes accidentally sting swimming humans.

Leopard sea anemones

Sea ferns and hydroids are made up of groups of tiny animals. Their "feathery" fronds cause a burning sting. Anemones are often called "sea flowers" but they are animals with stinging tentacles.

Magnificent hydroid

War wounds

Bluebottle

The bluebottle is also known as the Portuguese man-o-war and is sometimes mistaken for a sea jelly. It is really made up of many tiny animals, called hydrozoans, attached to a float (which is also an animal). Its main stinging tentacle can reach 10 metres long and a sting from it causes burning pain, blisters and welts.

My tentacles are toxic...

Box jelly

Sea jellies like the box jelly and the Irukandji don't look as fierce as sharks or crocodiles, but these wobbly little sea critters have caused far more deaths. In Australia, the box jelly has taken 67 lives over the past 80 years — that is more than any other animal. Irukandji and box jellies are highly venomous and are common in tropical waters from October to April.

Box jelly

Home & host

A sea anemone's stinging parts (or nematocysts) help it scare away predators, but some animals are able to avoid its sting. Anemonefish cover their bodies in the same type of slime (called mucus) that covers the sea anemone, which tricks it into thinking the fish is a part of its body, so the fish doesn't get stung. In return for a home, the anemonefish fights off butterflyfish, which eat anemones. This special relationship works for both fish and anemone.

Blackback anemonefish

IN OCEANS & RIVERS
URCHINS, STARS & CUCUMBERS

Pretty but prickly

Cake urchin

Some of the most spectacular sea creatures are the colourful animals named echinoderms (which means spiny skin). The group includes sea urchins, sea stars and sea cucumbers. Many have long needle-like spines and some are even venomous. While no sea stars or sea urchins have caused deaths in Australia, they can cause a lot of pain.

Ijima's fire urchin

Sea cucumber

Most sea cucumbers are harmless, but some seep out toxic mucus that can irritate the skin. Sea urchins, however, can cause cuts and stabs that may get infected.

False flowers

Although flower sea urchins look like a bunch of colourful blooms, if "picked" they would cause intense pain. Hidden among their spiny "flowers" are small, pincer-like parts attached to sacs of venom, which can sting without even splitting the skin.

Flower sea urchin

Most sea stars are harmless, but some have toxic spines that can pierce the skin. The most dangerous is the crown-of-thorns sea star, which eats coral and has 21 venomous and spiky "arms". This one is being eaten by a giant triton shell, one of this sea star's few predators.

Crown-of-thorns sea star

Worm Wounds

While the worms that you dig up in the backyard, or keep in worm farms, are harmless, some "bristle"-covered marine worms can cause harm to humans. Fire worms have very thin, very sharp, venomous spines down the side of the body that can even pierce rubber gloves.

Fire worm

IN & AROUND CREEKS & STREAMS

Frogs, toads, yabbies & more

Northern corroboree frog

Peron's tree-frog

Leech

Even some frogs use poison to kill animals that try to eat them. Touching frogs may also cause skin irritations. Other critters that hide in creeks and streams can also nip, scratch or even suck blood. Leeches like to live in boggy, mossy areas around creeks. They can latch on to skin and use their sucker-like mouths to "fill up" on blood.

The bright colours of the northern corroboree frog warn that it is toxic. Its toxin is mild to humans but may sting the skin.

Peron's tree-frogs secrete, or seep, toxins out of their skin. The toxins give them an odd musty smell. It is best not to touch frogs as you may also spread diseases to their skins.

Death on the hop

Cane toad

Cane toads, which were introduced to Australia to eat cane beetles, are among the most poisonous amphibians. Touching their warty, toxin-covered skin then touching your eyes or mouth can make you sick. Cane toads have killed many native animals that have eaten them thinking they are harmless frogs.

Freshwater crayfish

Freshwater crayfish, like their relatives the marine crayfish, lobsters and crabs, also have pincers, or claws, that help them catch and eat prey. They can grow very large and are covered in prickly spines that can scratch skin. You can safely pick up crayfish, like crabs, from the back of the body, avoiding the snapping claws.

Don't spur me on

The platypus is a very odd mammal! It is one of just two types of monotreme in Australia (the other is the echidna) and spends a lot of its time underwater in creeks and streams. As well as a duck bill and webbed feet, the male platypus has a sharp venomous spine, or spur, on its hindlegs. It may be used to fight other males or simply for protection.

Platypus

ON LAND
LIZARDS & PYTHONS

Snapping or squeezing

Frilled lizard

Perentie

Australia has a lot of large reptiles, but not all of them are dangerous in the way you might think. Not all snakes are venomous, for instance. Pythons are huge snakes, but they rarely bite. Instead, they squeeze their prey to death. Large monitor lizards, like the perentie, may hiss and run at a person and will bite and scratch if frightened.

The perentie is the largest lizard in Australia and can grow up to 2 metres long. It belongs to the monitor lizard, or goanna, family — a group of lizards that got their name from their habit of standing on their back legs to check (or monitor) their surroundings.

Recently scientists found that many monitor lizards and blue-tongue lizards have venom in their saliva, but it is not strong enough to cause serious harm to humans. Although, the perentie, like many large Australian lizards, has strong claws and can bite and scratch if afraid.

Bluff & bluster

Most lizards try to bluff, or trick, their way out of danger. They may stand up to their full height, hiss, and even poke out their tongues (like a blue-tongue) or puff out a frill (like the frilled lizard). If you stand your ground and look bigger too by putting your arms above your head, most lizards will scurry away rather than attack.

Olive python

I squeeze my prey until it can't breathe.

Carpet python

Swallowed whole!

A python wraps the thick coils of its body around its prey to squeeze, or constrict, it until it can no longer breathe. It then swallows its prey headfirst and whole. Sometimes a python may swallow a large animal that takes a long time to digest, like a chicken, and may not need to eat again for weeks!

ON LAND
VENOMOUS SNAKES

Eastern taipan

Snakes: deadly biters

Although there are some harmless snake species in Australia, this country also has the highest number of venomous snakes. Many of the world's deadliest snakes are found here, but most hide from humans.

Tiger snake

Death adder

It is hard to say which is the deadliest snake because some snakes with strong venom, like the western taipan, have caused few deaths, while less venomous snakes, like the tiger snake, have caused many.

Death adders have a very bad name, but are mostly shy snakes that bite when they are mistakenly stepped on. These snakes hide in sand, leaves and grass, twitching the tips of their tails to attract curious prey.

A serious striker

Australia's most feared snake is the coastal taipan. It has killed at least six people and strikes very fast, many times, to inject its venom. If annoyed, it can get very angry, but it would rather stay away from humans. The best way to avoid attack is to leave snakes alone and hurry away in the other direction if you see one.

Coastal taipan

Rough-scaled snake

Snakes use their tongues to "taste" the air or feel small movements, or vibrations, in the ground. They will often hear (or feel) you coming and slither away to safety.

We use our forked tongues to "taste" the air!

Spotted black snake

Fanging it

Venomous snakes are only able to bite so successfully thanks to their long fangs at the front of the mouth. Fangs work a little like a syringe or needle. They are hollow and are filled with venom from small sacs, or glands, of venom at the back of a snake's head (beneath the eye). Sometimes, if a snake has just bitten prey, its bite might not have any venom in it. This is known as a "dry" bite.

Death adder fangs

ON LAND
VENOMOUS SNAKES

Dangerous in doses

King brown snake

Some very dangerous snakes are no longer thought to be deadly, because people who have been bitten by these snakes usually live if they get to hospital quickly. Dangerous venomous snakes include some well-known snakes such as the red-bellied black snake, as well as others that are rarely seen in the wild.

Collett's snake is a beautiful coloured snake that belongs to the black snake family. Although it is venomous, it lives in bush habitat in central Queensland, where it rarely sees humans, so it hasn't been known to kill anyone. Many snakes that are dangerous live in out-of-the-way, or remote, places that humans don't often visit.

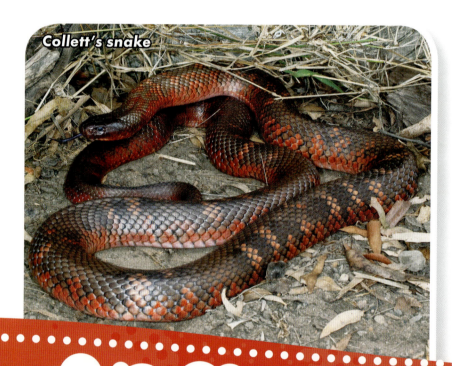
Collett's snake

Milking venom

Milking snakes

In the olden days, a bite from a snake was far more deadly than it is now. That is because scientists have been able to use snake venom to create a "cure", or antivenom, for some snakes' bites. To make antivenom, they "milk" the venom out of the snake's fangs by making it bite into a container. They then use it to make antivenom.

Red-bellied black snake

Small-eyed snake

Snakes alive!

You might have heard some people say "the only good snake is a dead snake". Many people used to try to kill snakes and thought of them as evil, instead of understanding that snakes are just wild animals protecting themselves the only way they know how. It is now against the law to kill snakes. People who try to kill or injure snakes may get bitten, so leave snakes alone and respect their right to life.

ON LAND
BIG BIRDS

Feathered fury

Australia has two species of large, flightless birds — the emu and the southern cassowary. Both can chase and hurt humans if they feel under attack. Even large waterfowl like swans and geese can get very angry if you try to get too close to their nests.

The emu is the second-largest bird in the world, after the ostrich. It is a curious bird that often approaches humans and will sometimes peck at bright buttons, shiny jewellery or belt buckles. Emus have powerful legs and are excellent runners. If a human threatens its nest or eggs, an emu may chase its attacker swiftly and peck at them with its sharp beak or scratch and kick out with its strong legs and toes.

Emu eggs and chick

Emu

Black swan

Black swan

Don't touch!

Swans, geese and other waterfowl don't like humans being near their eggs. They may hiss, ruffle up their feathers, chase a person or strike out and peck. It is best not to try to touch swans or geese.

Southern cassowary

Cassowary claws

Large cassowaries live in Queensland's rainforests. Like emus, they cannot fly and have muscular legs with large, clawed feet. They use their feet to scratch in the leaf litter to find food. However, they can also use them to kick out hard and scratch at humans who are bothering them. Like all wild animals, they should not be fed by humans, as they may get angry and attack when you take the food away.

Helmet head

The hard helmet-like bump on a cassowary's head is not a horn and is not used to headbutt people. It is known as a casque and is a spongy headpiece used to push through the rainforest vines. When cassowaries nest, it is the father cassowary who looks after chicks for many weeks. It is best to stay well away from their eggs, nests and young.

ON LAND
SPIDERS & OTHER CREEPY CRAWLIES

Small but deadly

Scorpion

Paralysis tick

Centipede

Small animals can be even more deadly than large ones, and spiders are a good example. Spiders, scorpions, centipedes and ticks like to hide under bark, in bushes or grass, or in burrows in the ground, and might go unseen until they bite. Not all are deadly, but some are.

The venomous paralysis tick has caused death to humans and pets. Ticks can also pass on diseases to humans.

Centipedes' toxic bites can cause swelling, pain and skin irritations, but, like scorpions, they are not deadly.

Funnelweb spider

The deadliest...

The male Sydney funnelweb spider is the deadliest spider known to man. Funnelwebs live in burrows near silken trap lines, which they build to catch prey. When they feel struggling prey, they rush out and bite it. Thirteen people died from this spider's bite before an antivenom was made in 1980.

Australian tarantula

I rear up to strike my prey!

Fatal females

People are afraid of red-back spiders lurking in outback toilets, sheds or other dark places, but red-backs are not as deadly as they seem. Only the females are deadly to humans; the males have small fangs that cannot pierce the skin. Since 1956, when an antivenom was made, no-one has died from a red-back bite.

Red-back spider

ON LAND
MAMMALS

Boxing, biting & stampeding

Red kangaroo

Water buffalo

Wild mammals can kill or injure humans through scratching, kicking, biting or headbutting. Introduced wild buffalo can chase and gore humans with their large horns. Feral pigs have sharp tusks that can gouge skin and sows are very protective of piglets. Even kangaroos are able to box and kick with harmful results.

Feral pig

Many of Australia's wild mammals are not native to this country but were brought here by early settlers. Feral pigs and buffalos are not only dangerous, they also dig up and damage rivers and creeks, and may carry diseases that can infect native animals.

Paws for thought

The dingo arrived in Australia about 4000 years ago, long before European settlers. Just like any dog, it is able to scratch, bite and even kill humans. While there have been two deadly dingo attacks on humans, there have been many more people killed by attacks from pet dogs. Treat dingoes like wild dogs and don't try to feed them, touch them or play with them.

Dingo

Red kangaroo

Kangaroo claws

kicking kangas

Roos are mostly gentle animals, but fully grown red kangaroos can be as large as a person and can have very large muscles, long claws and strong legs. Roos often fight, or box, each other in the wild. Their powerful kicks and sharp claws can tear open a person's stomach and cause awful injuries, although only one person has died from a kangaroo attack in Australia.

ON LAND & IN THE AIR
DISEASE-CARRYING MAMMALS

Cats, rats & bats

Bat

Some mammals can carry and spread disease, either by their bite, in their saliva, blood, wee or poo, or in germs or parasites that live on or in their bodies. Some of these diseases can be fatal to humans and may also kill other animals.

In the past, rats have spread many diseases through human cities and towns. Although Australia's native rats and mice mostly live in the aridlands, grasslands or woodlands, some feral rodents, like the house mouse and black rat, live in human sheds and houses where they scavenge food.

Rats infested with fleas helped spread the plague, which killed many people in the olden days. The fleas passed the disease from the blood of the rats to the blood of the people they jumped on and bit.

House mouse

Brown rat

Dalmatian

Feral cat

Pets & pests

Both feral and domestic dogs and cats can spread diseases to humans. Cats can carry the deadly disease toxoplasmosis, while dogs and cats can also pass on parasitic worms and other tiny, harmful germs on their skin. That's why you shouldn't kiss your pets and you should wash your hands after patting them or playing with them.

Little red flying-foxes

Bats can also pass viruses on to humans, but most people don't come into contact with these night-active mammals. If a bat bites a person, it might spread diseases such as lyssavirus (a rabies-like disease), Hendra virus or Menangle virus. To avoid being bitten, never touch or pick up a bat in the wild.

Grey-headed flying-fox

Yellow-bellied sheath-tail bat

Bottle-fed bats

Baby flying-fox

The chances of you getting bitten by a bat are low. Bats are very important to our environment because they help pollinate flowers and trees, so if you find an injured bat, don't touch it but quickly telephone a wildlife care network. They will take it to a carer or a "bat hospital" where injured or orphaned baby bats are looked after.

IN THE AIR & TREES
BIRDS

Corellas

Corellas

Attack from the air...

Danger and disease can also come from above. Birds are lovely, colourful animals, but many will swoop down on anything that threatens their nest. Birds can also carry lice and bacteria that can spread disease.

But don't be alarmed — just about any species that lives close to humans can spread disease. Birds such as parrots, cockatoos and even domestic chickens and geese can carry bacteria that can cause food poisoning. Cockatoos and parrots may also spread a disease called psittacosis. However, many people keep birds as pets and are not harmed.

If you do keep birds, remember to keep their roosts and feeding areas clean, change their water regularly and wash your hands after touching them. You can also buy powders and medicines to prevent the birds getting lice or parasites.

Galahs

Bird bugs

Chicken

Many people are scared of diseases that can cross from animals to humans, such as bird flu and swine flu. Just as humans may get the flu, other animals do too. Sometimes these other types of flu can begin to infect humans. Australia is good at controlling flu viruses, but just in case, stay away from sick or dead birds, cover your mouth when you sneeze and wash your hands after touching animals.

Almost everyone has been swooped by a magpie at some time in their lives. Magpies swoop to protect their territory and chicks, and their hard beaks can cause a nasty peck wound.

Australian magpie

Magpie swooping

Keep away when I am nesting.

Swoop & scratch

Masked lapwings fiercely defend the eggs they lay in grassy nests. They nest in pairs and are known for swooping down on people who walk past, to scare them away from the nest. Lapwings have slicing spurs that stick out from the front of their wings, and can stab or scratch an intruder as they swoop and peck.

Masked lapwing

IN THE AIR & TREES
GERMS, FLIES & MOSQUITOES

Disease in Flight

Fly

Illnesses can also come on the wing or even on the wind. Some germs float through the air and others may be carried on the tiniest insects. It is important to remember that mosquitoes, flies and cockroaches can be more dangerous disease carriers than most other, larger animals.

Many of the things that make humans sick are so small they can only be seen under a microscope. These "germs" are really tiny living things called bacteria or viruses, and when some types of "bad bacteria" or viruses get inside your body, they can make you ill.

However, there are many other types of "good bacteria" that live in our bodies every day and cause us no trouble at all — some even help us to fight infection or to digest food.

Microscope

Mouldy bread

 Flies, Fleas & lice

Bushfly

Flies and fleas land on humans and bite them. Australia has many species of biting fly, such as the march fly, but flies can also spread disease by landing on dung or garbage and then on food or humans' faces and bodies. Lice and fleas also live on humans and can cause itchy bites as well as disease. The deadly disease typhus was caused by bacteria passed on in lice bites.

Native cockroach

Cockroaches are scavengers that like to eat rotting food. Most of Australia's native cockroaches live in the bush, where they are not a threat to humans, but four kinds of non-native cockroach can infest houses and can spoil food and spread germs.

Introduced "Australian" cockroach

Bloodsuckers

Out of all animals, tiny mosquitoes have caused more human deaths than any other creature. They feed on human blood and can transmit, or pass on, diseases such as malaria, dengue fever and Ross River virus to those they bite. Mosquito bites can also be itchy and cause discomfit, but the viruses are most life threatening.

Mosquitoes

IN THE AIR & TREES
BEES, BEETLES & BUGS

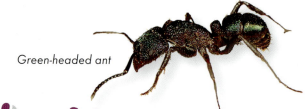
Green-headed ant

Small but painful stingers

Paper wasps
European honey bee

Most people have likely been bitten by an ant, wasp or bee at some time in their lives and found the sting mildly painful. But some people can have very serious allergic reactions to insect stings and may need to carry medicine with them in case of a sting.

Paper wasps live together in large paper-like nests, which they defend angrily if threatened. Only the female wasps have stings.

Some large, predatory bugs such as assassin bugs and the giant water bug can give humans a nasty nip in the garden.

Assassin bug
Giant water bug

BUZZ OFF

Some Australian native bees don't sting at all, but honey bees may sting if they feel under attack. Stinging is really a desperate act for a bee, because when they sting they die. Despite the cost, bees will sting to protect their colony or if they are stood on accidentally.

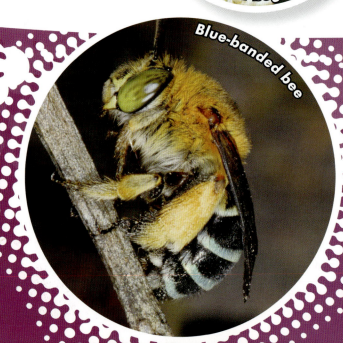
Blue-banded bee

Bull ant

I attack intruders that are much **bigger** than me!

Processionary caterpillar

Soldier beetle

Itchy bugs & biters

Most bugs and beetles are harmless, but some can be poisonous if eaten and others have strong jaws, called mandibles, that can give a sharp nip. The caterpillars of some butterflies may also be covered in small "itchy" hairs that can irritate humans' skin if they are touched.

FIRST AID

How to help yourself

Snake venom detection kit

If you or someone in your family is bitten or injured by a deadly or dangerous animal, the first thing to do is make sure no-one else will get hurt, so move well away from the danger before starting first aid. It is also good to know how you can help until you get to hospital or to a doctor. Different types of injury need different treatments.

CROCODILES, SHARKS OR DOGS

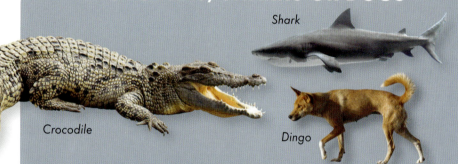

Shark
Crocodile
Dingo

For cuts, wounds, bites and scratches from crocodiles, sharks or dogs, the first thing to do is to keep calm and still and stop any bleeding. Keep the edges of the wound held tightly together and wrap a bandage firmly around the wound (but not so tight that it hurts). If the wound is on an arm or a leg, holding the limb up in the air will also help slow down the blood flow. Above all, phone 000 and get an ambulance to hospital immediately.

BLUE-RINGED OCTOPUS, CONE SHELL OR FUNNELWEB SPIDER

Blue-ringed octopus
Funnelweb spider
Cone shell

If you are stung by a cone shell, blue-ringed octopus or funnelweb spider, you should also apply a pressure bandage, keep still and calm, and go straight to hospital.

fish stings

Venomous fish stings can cause agony (awful pain) and it is important to stop some of the pain so the person doesn't go into shock. Putting the bitten part of the body in hot water (but not so hot that it burns) can help reduce the pain. Painkiller tablets can also help. Never bandage a fish sting.

Estuarine stonefish

VENOMOUS SNAKE BITES

Tiger snake

For venomous snake bites, it is important to stop the venom flowing around the body. Anyone bitten by a snake should stay as still as possible and have a firm pressure bandage applied to the bitten area. Never wash the bite and never try to catch the snake. Instead, rush the victim to hospital, where doctors will test the wound site to find a suitable antivenom.

SPIDER BITES

Apart from funnelwebs and mouse spiders, spider bites should not be bandaged but should have an ice pack put on the bite. Then get the victim to hospital.

Red-back spider

BEE & WASP STINGS

Bee

For bee and wasp stings, remove the sting from the victim's body and put an ice pack on the sting or bathe it in icy water. If you know the person is allergic or if they start to struggle to breathe or show other signs of distress, you should ask if they carry an epipen or other medicine and rush them to hospital.

Wasp

BOX JELLIES OR OTHER SEA JELLIES

If you are stung by a sea jelly such as a box jelly or Irukandji, pouring vinegar over the sting can decrease the pain. Most importantly, get to hospital.

Box jelly

Stop the shock

Keeping people calm, warm and comfortable, and talking to them to reassure them they will be okay, may help stop them going into shock. Shock is a medical condition that can happen after trauma or injury. Make sure the person's clothes are loose, that they are warm, and that they stay still and keep breathing as normally as possible.

GLOSSARY

AGONY Extreme pain.

ALLERGIC Being very sensitive to some things, such as bee stings, dust or pollen. Some people can become very sick from allergic reactions.

AMBUSH To hide and attack by surprise.

ANTIVENOM A substance used to treat people who have been bitten by a venomous snake or spider.

BARBS Sharp, sometimes arrow-shaped, spikes that can pierce or puncture skin.

COLONY A group of the same kind of animal living together.

ENDANGERED At risk of becoming extinct or dying out.

EPIPEN A treatment that people who suffer from serious allergies can carry around with them in case they have an allergic reaction.

FANGS Sharp teeth made for tearing into flesh or, in the case of venomous snakes, injecting venom into prey.

HABITAT Where an animal or plant lives and grows.

MANDIBLES The biting mouthparts of some insects.

MARINE Relating to the sea.

MONOTREME A special type of mammal that lays eggs.

NATIVE Belonging to a country or region; not introduced.

PARALYSIS Loss of control over the body, usually resulting in being unable to move or breathe.

PARASITE An animal or plant that lives on or in another species.

PINCERS The sharp claws of crabs or yabbies.

POISON A toxin that, if eaten or absorbed into the body, can cause pain, illness or death.

POLLINATE To transfer pollen from the male to the female part of the plant.

PREY An animal that is hunted and eaten by another animal.

PREDATOR An animal that hunts and eats other animals.

SCAVENGE To look for and take food.

SPECIES A group of organisms that are the same type and can breed to make babies.

SPINES Hard, sharp spikes that can cause injury.

SPUR A sharp, hard spike.

TOXIN A substance harmful to humans.

VENOM A type of toxin produced in the body of some animals that can cause illness, injury or death if somehow injected in a victim.

VENOMOUS A plant or animal that uses venom to catch prey or scare away attackers.

VIRUS Like a germ that causes illness.